# This
# Dinosaur

Kate McGough

# Look at the dinosaurs!

**Pachycephalosaurus**
(pack-ee-sef-ah-lo-sor-us)

**Parasaurolophus**
(pa-ra-sor-o-loa-fus)

**Hypsilophodon**
(hip-sil-oa-fo-don)

**Barosaurus**
(ba-ro-sor-us)

**Gastonia**
(gas-toa-nee-a)

**Ankylosaurus**
(an-kigh-lo-sor-us)

**Stegosaurus**
(steg-a-sor-us)

**Velociraptor**
(vel-oss-i-rap-tor)

**Baryonyx**
(ba-ri-o-nix)

**Brachiosaurus**
(brack-ee-oa-sor-us)

**Triceratops**
(trigh-se-ra-tops)

**Tyrannosaurus rex**
(tigh-ran-a-sor-us rex)

3

# Horns

Look at this dinosaur.
This dinosaur has three horns
on its head.

Crash

This dinosaur has one horn on its head.

# Claws

Look at this dinosaur.
This dinosaur has big claws
on its hands.

rip

shred

6

This dinosaur has big claws
on its feet.

# Tails

This dinosaur has a club on its tail.

Crash bang

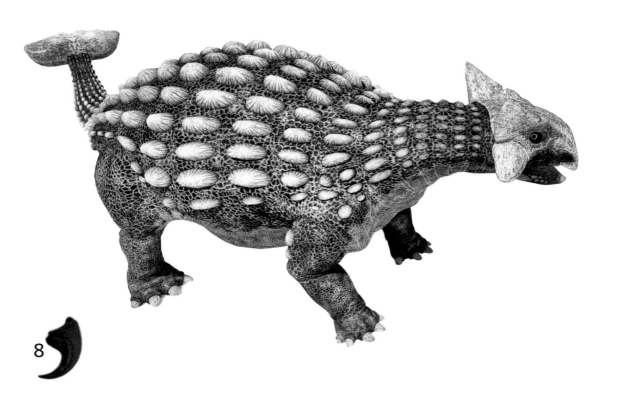

Look at this dinosaur.
It has a long, long tail!

# Spikes

This dinosaur has big spikes on its tail.

swish

bang

This dinosaur has lots of spikes on its back.

# Necks

This dinosaur has
a long neck.
It gets its food
from trees.

chomp

chomp

chomp

This dinosaur has a short neck and a strong head.

# Teeth

Look at this dinosaur.
This dinosaur has **big** teeth!
Its food is meat.

Run, little dinosaur, run!

chomp chomp chomp

# Picture Index